Kashimashi

~Girl Meets Girl~

OMNIBUS COLLECTION 1

story by
Satoru Akahori

art by
Yukimaru Katsura

P9-ASA-211

D0204082

Kashimashi
~Girl Meets Girl~
OMNIBUS COLLECTION 1

story by Satoru Akahori   art by Yukimaru Katsura
original character design Sukune Inugami

STAFF CREDITS

translation	**Adrienne Beck**
adaptation	**Janet Houck**
lettering	**Nicky Lim**
retouch	**Cheese**
layout	**Nicky Lim, Adam Arnold**
cover design	**Nicky Lim**
assistant editor	**Jason DeAngelis**
editor	**Adam Arnold**

Publisher   **Seven Seas Entertainment**

Kashimashi ~Girl Meets Girl~ Omnibus Collection I
© SATORU AKAHORI / YUKIMARU KATSURA 2005-2007
First published in 2005-2007 by Media Works Inc., Tokyo, Japan.
English translation rights arranged with Media Works Inc.

No portion of this book may be reproduced or transmitted in any
form without written permission from the copyright holders.

This is a work of fiction. Names, characters, places, and incidents
are the products of the author's imagination or are used fictitiously.
Any resemblance to actual events, locales, or persons, living
or dead, is entirely coincidental.

Seven Seas and the Seven Seas logo are trademarks of
Seven Seas Entertainment, LLC.

Visit us online at www.gomanga.com

ISBN: 978-1-934876-70-1

Printed in Canada

First Printing: June 2009

10 9 8 7 6 5 4 3 2 1

C O N T E N T S

Scenario: Satoru Akahori   Comic: Yukimaru Katsura
Original Character Design: Sukune Inugami
School Uniform Design: COSPA inc.

#1 The Day He Changed

OH...

#1 The Day He Changed

!

GO MAKE HER YOUR GIRL, HAZUMU! THEN YOU'LL BE A *REAL* MAN!

THIS IS THE *PERFECT* OPPORTUNITY THEN!

YEAH...

YEAH, HAZUMU! GO FOR IT!

SHAKE SHAKE

IF THAT DOES END UP BEING THE CASE...

COULD YOU HANDLE IT, HAZUMU-KUN?

THERE *IS* THE POSSIBILITY OF LOSING HER AS A FRIEND.

AND SHE SAYS NO...

BUT IF YOU DO ASK...

HAZUMU-KUN.

YASUNA-CHAN...

YOU DON'T H-HAVE TO GO OUT WITH ME I-IF YOU DON'T *WANT* TO.

I WON'T MIND.

B-BUT YOU DON'T *HAVE* TO...! ER... THAT IS...

BUT... IF YOU DON'T MIND--

SAY... N-NO...

AH...

Y-YOU CAN JUST...

IT'S OKAY!

B-THMP

B-THMP

I-I REALLY MEAN THAT. IF YOU... DON'T WANT TO, JUST FORGET I-I-I...UM, I MEAN...

HAZUMU-KUN...

IT DIDN'T TURN OUT FOR HIM THEN, HUH?

SO...

PROBABLY. BUT, YEAH...

・・・・・・・・・・

WHA?!

WH-WH-WHAT WOULD I BE *RELIEVED* FOR?!

そんなこと ないない That's not it at all!!

RE-LIEVED?

--AH.

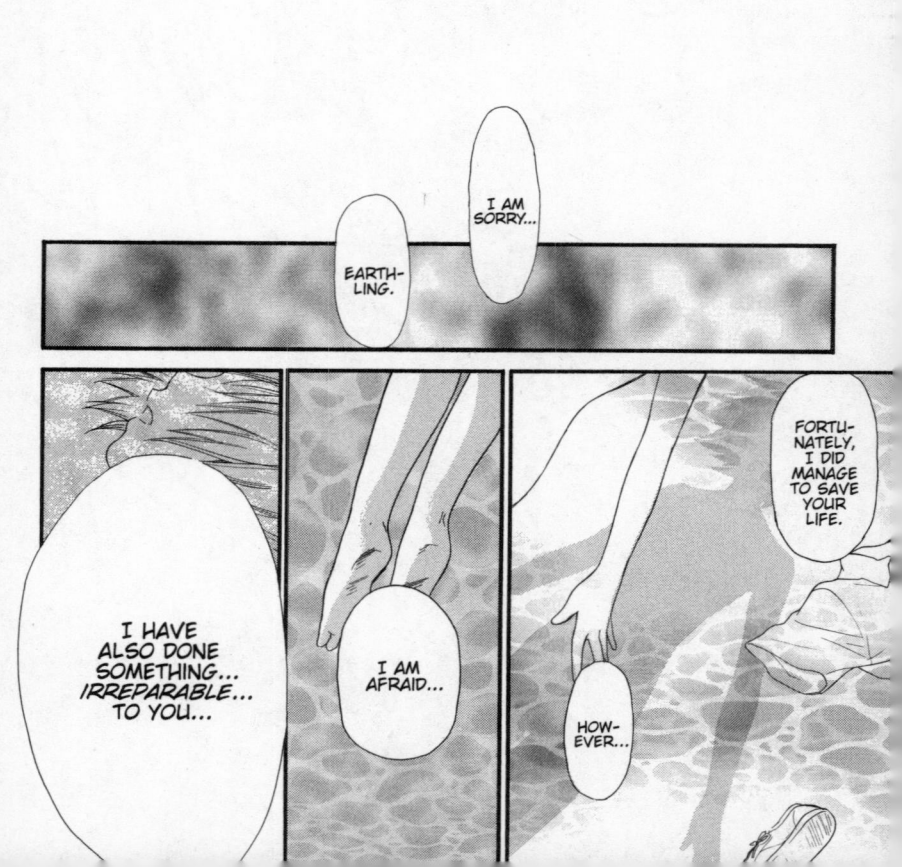

I AM SORRY...

EARTH-
LING.

I HAVE
ALSO DONE
SOMETHING...
IRREPARABLE...
TO YOU...

I AM
AFRAID...

HOW-
EVER...

FORTU-
NATELY,
I DID
MANAGE
TO SAVE
YOUR
LIFE.

BUT *THAT* HAS ALLOWED ME TO *DEVOTE* MY LIFE TO *TEACHING!*

I, TSUKI NAMIKO...

HAVE BEEN WITHOUT A BOY-FRIEND FOR THESE 35 *LONG* YEARS.

WHA?

NAMIKO-SENSEI?

S-SEN-SEI...?

Y-YES!

sensei sensei

AS *HIS* HOME-ROOM TEACHER...

I *SWEAR* THAT I WILL *BRING* YOUR PRECIOUS SON *HOME* TO YOU!

GABA!
SNAP

I HEARD POOR HAZUMU-KUN WAS *MISSING,* SO I *RUSHED* OVER HERE AS *FAST* AS MY *LEGS* COULD CARRY ME!

SWF

WHAAAAA--?!

DA
DASH!

NOW, I *MUST* BE OFF!!

#2 She Realized She Was A Girl

SIX HOURS HAVE PASSED SINCE THE SUDDEN AND SHOCKING ARRIVAL OF VISITORS FROM ANOTHER PLANET.

OSARAGI HAZUMU-SAN IS JUST NOW RETURNING TO HER HOME.

AS THE OTHER-WORLDLY BEING STATED, OSARAGI HAZUMU-SAN IS ENTIRELY FEMALE. IN RESPONSE TO THIS, PRIME MINISTER OHIZUMI...

AFTER AN EXHAUSTIVE BATTERY OF TESTS AT THE HOSPITAL, IT HAS BEEN CONCLUDED THAT...

Osaragi Hazumu-San (17)

HAS ANNOUNCED THAT TOMORROW, THE HOUSE OF REPRESENTATIVES' BUDGETARY COMMITTEE...

WILL BEGIN DELIBERATIONS ON WHETHER OR NOT TO CHANGE OSARAGI HAZUMU-SAN'S GENDER IN HER OFFICIAL FAMILY REGISTER FROM "MALE" TO "FEMALE."

#2
She Realized She Was A Girl

ARE YOU SURE YOU'RE OKAY WITH BEING A GIRL?

CRAMMED...

MOM...

I DON'T REALLY HAVE ANY CHOICE.

BUT...

I LOVE YOU.

NO ONE CAN CHANGE ME BACK, SO I HAVE TO GO ON...

AND LIVE OUT THE REST OF MY LIFE AS A GIRL.

I CAN'T.

I'M A GIRL NOW.

I--

PUU

HELLO THERE!

TWITCH

?!

HOW HAVE YOU BEEN, FORMER YOUNG MALE...

NO.

I MEAN, CURRENT YOUNG FEMALE?

ONEE-NII-SAMA!!!

THAT WE SHALL BE SHARING YOUR DOMICILE FOR THE FORESEEABLE FUTURE.

BUT YES, MOVING ALONG. I WANTED TO INFORM YOU...

FUU

IT'S A PLEASURE.

UH...

HUH?

FOR OBSERVATIONAL PURPOSES, OF COURSE.

WHAT?

WHAT THE HECK?!

#3 My First...

GIRLS LAVATORY

....

GOD!

HAZUMU!

UGH...

HURT YOURSELF WITH THAT STATEMENT, HMM?

YOU ARE A *GIRL* NOW!!

whisper whisper

UM...

WELL...

I DID BUY ONE.

I figured I probably had to wear one...

YOU DID?

?

GIRLS WEAR *BRAS!* GOT THAT?!

Panel 1:
TOMARI COULD FIT HER WHOLE HEAD IN ONE OF THESE CUPS.

It's huge!

WHY THE HELL DID YOU BUY *THIS* ONE?!

Panel 2:
WOW.

Panel 3:
BUT...

BAAAM ん!

Panel 4:
WELL, EVERYTHING WAS OKAY UNTIL I WALKED INTO THE STORE...

Panel 5:
THERE ARE OF TONS THEM!

HOW AM I SUPPOSED TO FIGURE OUT WHICH ONE TO BUY?

HOLY CRAP!

Panel 6:
I'LL TAKE THIS ONE!!

Panel 7:
UM...

I...

Panel 8:
SMILE

URK!

HELLO THERE. WOULD YOU LIKE FOR ME TO TAKE YOUR MEASURE-MENTS?

GOOD NIGHT.

SWAP

GLOOM...

ACCORDING TO MY STATISTICS, APPROXIMATELY 70% OF YOUNG EARTH FEMALES PURCHASE THE WRONG SIZE WHEN SHOPPING FOR THEIR FIRST BRASSIERE.

DING DONG

I- I WOULD LIKE TO HAVE SOMEONE WITH ME...

OOPS. BETTER HURRY. RECESS IS OVER.

HUH...? WHY *ME*?! CAN'T *YOU* GO?

NOPE. I HAVE CLUB.

BUT YOURS HAS TODAY OFF, RIGHT?

...I SEE.

TOMARI, WHY DON'T YOU GO WITH HI-- I MEAN, *HER* AFTER SCHOOL AND SHOW HER WHAT TO BUY?

WELL, THAT'S UNDER- STANDABLE.

TOMARI-CHAN, PLEASE?!

WHAT'S UP WITH YOU TWO?! YOU JUST SAW EACH OTHER AT SCHOOL TODAY, RIGHT?!
Uhhh...
Um...
CRAP. NOW WHAT DO I DO?
UMMM... OKAY... TALK ABOUT SOME-THING...
bathump
bathump
I LOVE YOU.
ACK!
SHE ACCIDENTALLY REMEMBERED!
SO... UM... YOU'RE GOING SHOPPING?
UH... YEAH!
OH MY...

THAT'S RIGHT...
YOU WOULD NEED ONE NOW, WOULDN'T YOU?
EH HEH HEH...
......
LET'S GO, HAZUMU.
GET YOURSELF MEASURED, GET A BRA, AND LET'S GET HOME, OKAY?
OH... UM... OKAY.
LATER.
......
THERE.
YOU'RE JUST AT...
70 CENTI-METERS. THAT'S A "C" CUP.
OH...
WOULD YOU LIKE TO TRY ON A FEW?
EEp
EEp
SHE'S BIGGER THAN ME...

THERE!

ALL DONE!

VERY CUTE.

YES.

· · · · · · · ·

OH?

I DIDN'T FEEL EMBAR-RASSED AT ALL ABOUT BEING *TOTALLY NAKED* A MINUTE AGO.

IT FEELS... REALLY WEIRD.

I FEEL... EMBAR-RASSED, ALL OF A SUDDEN.

DOES IT HURT AT ALL?

HOW DOES IT FEEL?

IT DOESN'T HURT, BUT...

THANKS,
TOMARI.

BOTH
YOU AND
YASUNA-CHAN
WERE A LOT
OF HELP.

HN.

HAZUMU.

ARE
YOU...
YOU
KNOW...
OKAY?

ABOUT
YASUNA.

YEAH.

SO I'M OKAY WITH IT.

BEFORE I CONFESSED TO HER, I DECIDED...

I'D STILL WANT TO GO BACK TO BEING FRIENDS...

IF THAT WAS OKAY WITH HER.

THAT EVEN IF SHE SAID NO...

OH. OKAY.

I'M A GIRL NOW.

BESIDES...

AND GIRLS CAN'T HAVE OTHER GIRLS AS GIRLFRIENDS.

ON THE DAY...

ANY POSSIBILITY THAT WE MIGHT BE SOMETHING MORE THAN FRIENDS... *VANISHED.*

THAT THIS BODY OF MINE CHANGED...

WHY WOULD SHE GO AND TELL ME SOMETHING LIKE *THAT* NOW? I DON'T GET IT.

I LOVE YOU.

KURUSU RESIDENCE

HE... SHE SAID SHE WAS OKAY, BUT WHAT IF SHE'S REALLY NOT?

I WONDER IF THAT *PUTZ* IS STILL EATING RIGHT.

IS SHE HAVING ANY OTHER PROBLEMS WITH HER NEW GIRL BODY...?

HMM... CAN H-- *SHE* GET THOSE NEW BRAS ON OKAY BY HERSELF?

--WAIT.

WHAT THE HELL AM *I* GETTING ALL WORRIED FOR?!!

GRAAK

SO WHY...

DO I GET THIS WEIRD FEELING IN MY CHEST WHENEVER I THINK ABOUT IT?

I KNOW THAT.

"GIRLS CAN'T HAVE OTHER GIRLS AS GIRLFRIENDS."

#4 Tomari, Confused!

#4 Tomari, Confused

CRYBABY! CRYBABY! HAZUMU'S A *CRYBABY!*

HA HA! HAZUMU ALWAYS CRIES!

DON'T LISTEN TO A WORD THOSE JERKS SAY, OKAY? IT'S ALL *LIES.*

HAZUMU...

LET'S GO SOME-WHERE ELSE.

HA HA! HE'S SO STUPID HE NEEDS TO HAVE A *GIRL* PROTECT HIM!

AAAH! THERE SHE IS!

RUN!

HEY! GET AWAY FROM HIM!!

SO YOU DON'T HAVE TO CRY ANYMORE.

I'LL PROTECT YOU.

TOMARI-CHAN, DO YOU HAVE A SEC?

TOMARI-CHAN! WHAT DO I DO WHEN--

OH NO! TOMARI-CHAN! WHAT DO I DO NOW?!

WOULD YOU SHUT UP ALREADY?!!

QUIT ASKING ME ABOUT *EVERY* TEENY TINY LITTLE THING!!!

ALTHOUGH, IF IT WAS ANY *OTHER* GUY-TURNED-GIRL, WE'D KICK HIM OUT IN A *HEARTBEAT!*

I MEAN, IT'S *HAZUMU-KUN.*

COME ON, TOMARI. WHAT'S THE BIG DEAL?

NOBODY HERE REALLY MINDS, RIGHT?

Let the poor girl change with us, okay?

CAN'T THEY JUST *SHUT UP?!*

YOU KNOW, HAZUMU-KUN REALLY *IS* CUTE.

WHAT, DOES IT BUG YOU?

BLUSH

OR SO SHE SAYS.

NO! IT DOESN'T!!

Oh. Is that so?

IT'S LIKE SHE'S *ALWAYS* BEEN A GIRL.

Hazumu-kun, that bra is so cute!

Really? Tomari-chan picked it out for me.

BATHUMP

O-KAY!! ♡

...daughters or sons are referred to as the "chasen-mage"

Of their parent's hair.

This phrase originates from Nobunaga, who is "o-tamake"...

OKAY. I'LL ADMIT HAZUMU'S CUTE. I MEAN...

EVEN FROM THE STANDPOINT OF ANOTHER GIRL, LIKE ME, IT'S EASY TO CALL H- HER "BEAUTIFUL."

EVERYBODY! ALL MY PRETTY STUDENTS!

LET'S STUDY ENGLISH REALLY HARD!

THAT WAS VERY *FEMININE*, THE WAY YOU DID THAT.

YOU KEPT YOUR KNEES TOGETHER.

OH, WOW...

REALLY...?

WELL, TOMARI-CHAN *DOES* ALWAYS YELL AT ME TO REMEMBER I'M IN A SKIRT.

GRR

HAZUMU! WE'RE GOING NOW!

UM... THAT I'D LIKE TO MAYBE...

GO TO LOOK AT THE PLANTS BACK ON THE MOUNTAIN AGAIN SOMETIME SOON.

I'LL SEE YOU LATER, HAZUMU-KUN.

OH? UM... OKAY. BYE.

THE PRESS WILL AMBUSH YOU UP THERE.

•••••

I KNOW, BUT... WELL...

HEY, TOMARI-CHAN.

AT GARDENING CLUB TODAY, I WAS KINDA THINKING...

•••••

FZT

ONEE-NII-SAMA!

WHAT THE HELL?!

SHE JUST... APPEARED OUT OF THIN AIR!!

FZT

The Alien's Explanation Corner

Let me explain the phenomenon you just observed. While levitating in the air, Jan-puu emits a special field that bends light around her. This renders her invisible to normal human vision, as well as any photographic devices, such as cameras. Hence, when she switches off the field, it seems as if she is suddenly appearing out of thin air!

FZT

FZT

Puu puu

SHE'S ONE OF THE SPACE ALIENS?!

YEAH...THEY DECIDED TO STAY AT MY HOUSE FOR SOME REASON.

WE EVEN TOOK A *BATH* TOGETHER *LAST* NIGHT! ♡

ONEE-NII-SAMA AND JAN-PUU ARE *BESTEST* BEST FRIENDS.♡ WE SLEEP TOGETHER *EVERY* NIGHT.

WELL... WE ARE *BOTH* GIRLS.

twitch

YOU WHAT?!

DON'T EVER TELL ANYONE ELSE THAT, OKAY?

O-OKAY...

"Onee-ni-sama?! What's up with that?"

ABSOLUTELY EVERYBODY'S TRYING TO MAKE *HAZUMU* INTO A GIRL!

ず
ん STOMP
す STOMP
ん

HE'S A GIRL ALL THE WAY DOWN TO HIS DNA NOW. WHO CARES?!

SO WHAT IF HE CAN'T EVER BE TURNED BACK INTO A BOY AGAIN!

IF EVERYONE KEEPS TRYING TO CHANGE EVERY LAST THING ABOUT HIM, THEN--

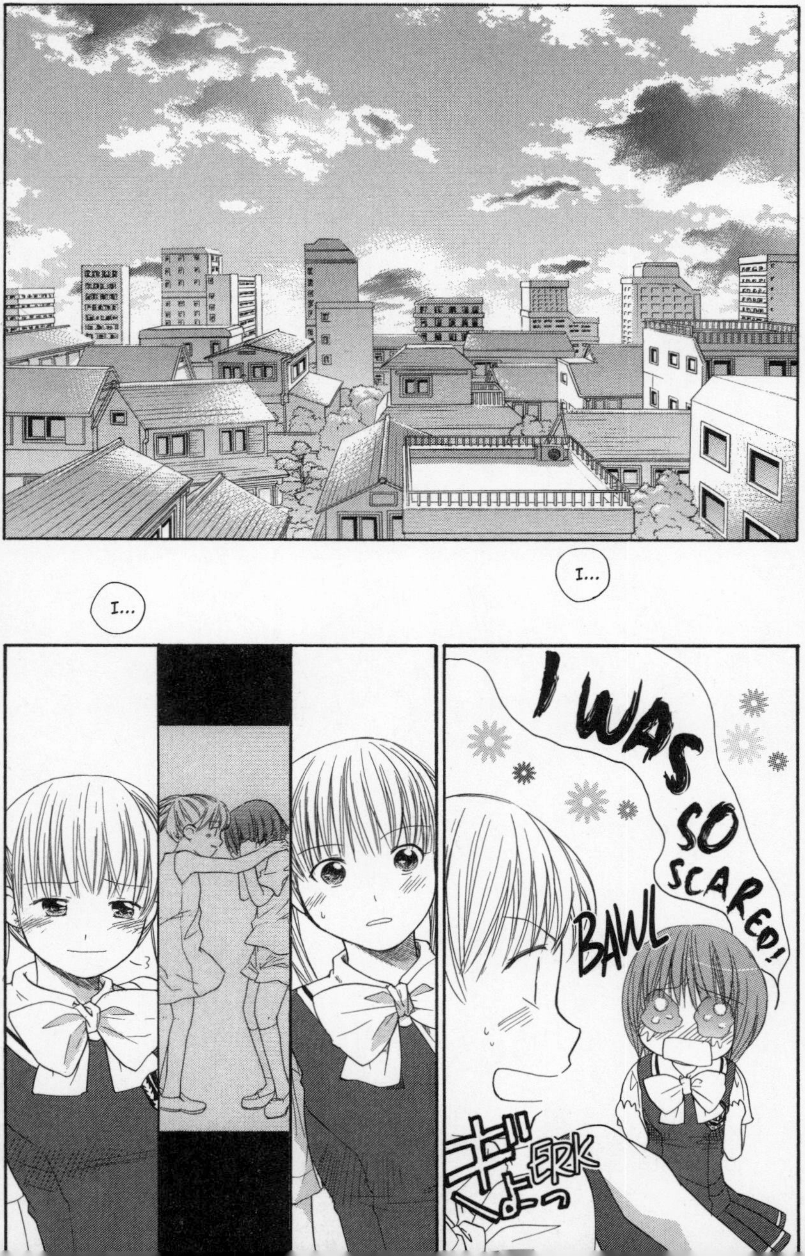
I...
I...
I WAS SO SCARED!
BAWL
ERK

...WHOA. WAIT A MINUTE!!

なんだこ ドレ !

WHAT THE HELL AM I DOING?!

?

ANYWAY! IT'S A MOTHER'S PROTECTIVE INSTINCTS I'M FEELING! THAT'S ALL! THAT'S IT! NOTHING ELSE!!

TO ME, HAZUMU IS LIKE A LITTLE BROTHER...UM, WELL, LITTLE SISTER NOW, I GUESS.

RO-MANTIC LOVE AT ALL!

Nee-chan, who are you talking to?

IT'S MOTHERLY LOVE!!

IT'S NOT R-... R-...

SHUT UP!

NOTHING WILL EVER CHANGE THAT. AT LEAST, I DON'T THINK SO, ANYWAY.

QUITE THE INTERESTING SPECIMEN, THIS HUMAN FEMALE.

munch munch

HMM.

#5
Hazumu's Heart

FWEET

I'M NOT KIDDING! IT WAS THE *COOLEST* THING *EVER*!!

QUIT TELLING EVERYBODY WHACKED OUT STORIES ABOUT WHAT HAPPENED.

BUT IT'S NOT ANYTHING BAD, TOMARI-CHAN. I'M *BRAGGING* ABOUT YOU!

UH, HAZU-MU...

THERE I WAS, SUR-ROUNDED BY A *MOB* OF RAVENOUS REPORTERS.

I THOUGHT I WAS A *GONER* FOR SURE! JUST WHEN I WAS ABOUT TO GIVE UP...

SQUEEE ♥

TOMARI-CHAN *FLIES* ONTO THE SCENE LIKE A SUPER-HERO! *LITERALLY*!

OH. HI...

I DIDN'T "TOSS" ANYBODY.

BEFORE WE GO ANY FURTHER, THERE *IS* SOMETHING EXTREMELY IMPORTANT I HAVE TO TELL YOU ALL.

SHE *RIPPED* INTO THE *EVIL* HORDE OF REPORTERS, *TOSSING* THEM AROUND LIKE--

OH MY GOD! TOMARI-CHAN!!

AYUKI!!

TOMARI ONCE RECEIVED A LOVE LETTER FROM A GIRL.

N-NO!! THAT'S NOT IT!! IT WAS A *FAN* LETTER! Y'SEE, ONE OF MY KOUHAI ON THE TRACK TEAM SAW ME DURING THIS ONE MEET AND--

NO WAY

MY PRINCE CHARMING 私の王子様...♥

AHHH! TOMARI, YOU'RE JUST SO COOL!

"what we're thinking?" What do you think we're thinking?

B-BUT IT'S NOT WHAT YOU'RE THINKING! THAT'S NOT IT AT ALL!!

AH!

That she did.

THEN YOU REALLY *DID* GET A LETTER...!

IF YOU WERE A BOY, I'D HAVE SUCH A *BIG* CRUSH ON YOU!

ANYWAY, NOT TO CHANGE THE TOPIC, BUT...

I'm going back to my club...

YEAH, SHE REALLY IS A DUDE...

I'm a girl, dammit!!

WHEN HAZUMU GROWS UP INTO A BIG GIRL, SHE'S GOING TO MARRY *DADDY*, RIGHT?

OH DEAR. ARE THERE... *PLANS* ALREADY?

SHE DOESN'T WANT TO HUG YOU, ASUTA.

NO!

OH MY GOD!

What was I doing?!

WONK WONK

AND MOM AND DAD SEEM REALLY HAPPY TO HAVE A *DAUGHTER* INSTEAD OF A SON...

SURE, MY BODY'S ENTIRELY FEMALE NOW...

JEEZ. WHAT'S GOTTEN INTO EVERY-BODY?

SO, IN OTHER WORDS, YOU STILL LIKE GIRLS...?

I DON'T KNOW...

--AH, WHO CARES?!

NOW ISN'T THE TIME TO BE THINKING ABOUT THAT KIND OF STUFF, ANYWAY!

...BUT MY HEART...

DOESN'T CHANGE SO EASILY.

WHEN I FIRST STARTED SCHOOL HERE, THERE WAS ONLY **ONE** TINY LITTLE FLOWERBED UP HERE.

THE MUSIC ROOM IS RIGHT OVER THERE.

IT'S VERY EASY TO SEE THIS ROOF WHEN I'M THERE FOR PRACTICE.

IT USED TO BE SUCH A **DREARY** VIEW, THIS ROOFTOP.

I CAME TO LOVE LOOKING AT THIS GARDEN.

UNTIL A RAINBOW OF **COLORS** WOULD CHANGE WITH THE SEASON.

BUT WHEN YOU CAME, THE GREENERY JUST GREW AND GREW...

AND I...
UM...

YOU KNOW,
HAZUMU-
KUN...

LISTENED
ALL THE
TIME.

T-TO
YOUR
FLUTE,
I MEAN.

YOU HAVE
THE POWER
TO MAKE
THE WORLD
BEAUTIFUL.

HAZUMU-KUN...

GASHA

UH...?

THERE YOU ARE!

AHA!

HEY!! HAZUMUUU!

LET'S GO, ASUTA!

HUH?

WHA?

TWITCH

WILL I EVER FALL IN LOVE AGAIN?

I, TSUKI NAMIKO, HAVE NEVER HAD A BOYFRIEND IN ALL 35 *LONG* YEARS OF MY LIFE.

BUT I WILL *NOT* FEAR! I WILL *NOT* SHRINK FROM THE CHALLENGE! I *WILL* LOVE!!

#6 What Yasuna Sees

ASLEEP OR AWAKE, I CAN'T STOP THINKING ABOUT HAZUMU-KUN.

I'M SO STRANGE...

SQUEEZE

WELL, PERHAPS YOUR BLOOD PRESSURE *IS* A BIT LOW.

BLOOD PRES-SURE...

PULSE RATE...

NORMAL.

BY THE BY...

WHICH ONE WILL YOU CHOOSE?

HUH?

WHAT-EVER THIS MACHINE IS, IT'S *REALLY* RETRO!

ON MY WORLD, ANTIQUES HAVE BECOME *QUITE* POPULAR.

I AM REFERRING TO YOUR *FUTURE* ROMANTIC PARTNER.

KAMIIZUMI YASUNA OR KURUSU TOMARI, WHICH ONE WILL YOU CHOOSE?

ずGAKばっ

PUUUUU!!

HM?

※ ☆
● □
△
!! ▼

BECAUSE... BECAUSE...

ONEE-NII-SAMA IS GOING TO MARRY *JAN-PUU*!

HUH?

ONEE-NII-SAMA WAS JAN-PUU'S FIRST *KISS*.

BLUSH

WHEN WE FIRST MET... IN THE MOUNTAINS!

ЄЄЄ ♥

ARE YOU NOT INTER-ESTED IN *ROMANCE?*

N-NO... THAT'S NOT IT.

UM...BUT ANYWAY, RIGHT NOW...

PUUU

I'M NOT TRYING TO PICK ANY... UM... PARTNERS...

YOU DEFINI-TIVELY HAVE AFFECTIONATE FEELINGS FOR *BOTH* FEMALES.

ACCORDING TO MY OB-SERVATIONS...

BESIDES...

I'M A GIRL NOW.

THAT'S BECAUSE THEY'RE MY *FRIENDS!*

I SEE. GO ON.

UMM...

YEAH...?

UHH...

BONK

IS THERE ANYONE YOU...

WELL, YOU KNOW... LIKE?

Besides, Hazumu did used to be a guy and all... Well, no, maybe I shouldn't think of her as a "former-him." That's not really fair. Whoa...wait a second...THAT'S IT! THAT'S PRECISELY IT!! NO. THEY CAN'T!! So, as Hazumu's best friend, it's my DUTY... and pleasure... to accept her burgeoning feelings for me!!!

whrrr whrrr

SNIK Grind Grind Grind Grind

WHAT THE HELL?! what does she mean by that?! NO WAY!! Is she trying to tell me that she... she...! Oh my god!! I've gotta be the luckiest guy in the world!!! NO, NO, NO, NO! WAIT! I'm such an idiot! Hazumu and me are friends! FRIENDS! That's it!

?

THIS **SPECIMEN** IS A GENETICALLY ALTERED PLANT THAT YOU CALL "SUNFLOWER."

THANK YOU.

AS THE PLANT IS **HARMFUL**, BE CAREFUL **NOT** TO BECOME ENSNARED.

I- IT SPOKE...!!

YOU LEAD A MOST INTRIGUING CLASS, SENSEI.

KAMIIZUMI-SAN?

COULD YOU HAND ME THAT BEAKER?

OH...

--WHAT? IS THIS SPECIMEN **THAT** TERRIBLY RARE?

FROM MY OBSERVATIONS, I PRESUMED THIS TO BE A COMMON, WELL-LOVED TOY.

SENSEI, THAT'S A MACHINE!!!

WONDERFUL! IT'S A DATE THEN!

UH...

SURE.

HUH?

I'D BE VERY GRATEFUL IF YOU WOULD BE MY GUIDE.

IT'S ON KASHIMA MOUNTAIN.

IS REALLY FUN FOR ME.

JUST BEING NEAR YASUNA-CHAN...

BUT IS THAT REALLY LOVE?

I DON'T KNOW ANYMORE.

I STILL GET A LITTLE FLUSTERED WHEN I'M AROUND YASUNA-CHAN.

THERE YOU ARE!

SORA-SENSEI!!

THEN LET US BE ON OUR WAY, SORA-SENSEI!

YES?

PLEASE! ALLOW ME, TSUKI NAMIKO, TO GIVE YOU THE **GRAND** TOUR OF OUR **WONDERFUL** SCHOOL!

OH, HAZUMU-KUN!

UM, SURE.

WOULD YOU BE A DARLING AND STOP BY THE ART ROOM TO PICK UP LAST YEAR'S ART CONTEST ENTRIES?

IF SHE DOES, IT IS ONLY AS UNDEFINED, INORGANIC OBJECTS.

KAMIIZUMI YASUNA DOES NOT APPEAR TO VISUALLY RECOGNIZE MALES, SUCH AS MYSELF.

WHAT THE HECK...?

#7 Girl Triangle

WHY DON'T YOU LET YOUR DEAR OLD *DADDY* JOIN YOU IN A *BIG, WARM* BUBBLE BATH? THERE'S NOTHING WRONG WITH A BUBBLE BATH, IS TH--

OH, HAZUMU!

ロー/バタ゛ソバババゖ!
ROUNDHOUSE KICK

ARE YOU SPOUTING THAT **CRAP** AGAIN?! **GIVE UP ALREADY**!!

WAAAAAH! CAN'T I AT LEAST DREAM?

. . . .

#7
Girl Triangle

THE FACE WASN'T DETAILED...

BUT THAT WAS STILL ME.

THAT PICTURE YASUNA-CHAN DREW...

WOW...

BLUSH

WE BEGAN TO LOSE ALL SEXUAL URGES.

HOW-EVER, THERE *WERE* SIDE EFFECTS.

BY BECOMING A CALM, RATIONAL AND LOGICAL RACE...

EMOTIONAL CLASHES, SUCH AS VIOLENCE AND WAR, DISAPPEARED ENTIRELY.

BUT IN SO DOING, WE ALSO ELIMINATED ALL SOURCES OF INTENSE CONNECTION.

WE ELIMINATED ALL SOURCES OF INTENSE REPULSION BETWEEN OURSELVES.

IT WILL NOT BE LONG BEFORE WE ARE COM-PLETELY EXTINCT.

SHOULD OUR CURRENT SITUATION CONTINUE...

OUR SOCIETY BECAME ONE WITHOUT CONFRONTATIONS. OUR WORLD BECAME ONE OF *PERFECT* PEACE.

THE ONE SOLUTION AT WHICH I HAVE ARRIVED IS--

·········

YEAH.

THIS IS MY FAVORITE SPOT.

SO MANY "FUKI."

ISN'T THIS ALSO THE PLACE WHERE WE MET?

YEAH.

GRRRR

OH...

WE'D BETTER GET TO DRAWING.

OH MY...

CHIRP CHIRP CHIRP

CLASSMATES, TEACHERS, THE PEOPLE I'M AROUND EVERY DAY, IT DOESN'T MATTER... I HAVE *NEVER* SEEN THEM.

FOR A LONG TIME, I THOUGHT THAT IF MY CONDITION NEVER CHANGED...

IF I WERE STUCK LIKE THIS FOR THE REST OF MY LIFE, I'D NEVER BE ABLE TO FIND LOVE.

THEN...

I MET YOU, HAZUMU-KUN.

YOU WERE THE *FIRST* BOY I COULD EVEN *VAGUELY* SEE.

Bonus Track

She's in the Woodwind Ensemble.

This is Yasuna-chan.

She's on the Track Team.

This is Tomari-chan.

This is Ayuki-chan. She's...

I'm in the Gardening Club.

Hi! I'm Hazumu.

Ayu—

Ayuki-chan...!

What's with the huge sacks?!

They look really heavy!

DRAGDRAGDRAG ← YIKES

Ha ha ha...

REASON

Heh heh. Never would've worn this frilly stuff when you were a boy, huh?

. . . . .

↑ Got changed

REASON

They're way more comfortable.

But personally, I like boys' clothing a lot better.

Tomari looks rather... concerned about you.

She let me have a black bookbag, though, just like the other boys.

Mom always says gender discrimination isn't a good thing.

Wow...

↑ Has been a dress-up doll ever since then...

Puu-puu.

Pu.

Puu. puu

pu

puu

PUUUUU!!

What?

Pupuu!

What's wrong, Jan-puu-chan?

Puu puu!

Jan-puu is so cute! She looks like a big, fluffy dumpling.

Hm? I was under the impression that she would be more "moe" if incapable of proper speech.

CHANGE HER BACK!

MONEY MONEY

Puuuu

DENGEKI DAIOH

DENGEKI DAIOH

DENGEKI DAIOH

DENGEKI D

DENGEKI D

Apologies for the disjointedness of Chapters 1~7. These characters are supposed to be in high school, but in Chapter 1, it feels like they should be junior high schoolers! On another note, I recently learned to appreciate high school girls. They have such great thighs!

#8 Bride and Groom

TO-TOMARI-CHAN!

WSH

AH!

にぱ
SMILE
HEH HEH...
SORRY...
I... DIDN'T MEAN TO INTERRUPT YOU.
SO...
I GUESS... THE FEELING IS MUTUAL THEN, HUH?
......
UH...
ER...
......
HUH.
WOW... THAT'S... GREAT.

LATER!

TOMARI-CHAN!!

UM...

JUST... GREAT.

TO--

FOR ACCEPTING ME.

THANK YOU...

AFTER THAT DAY...

YASUNA-CHAN STARTED WALKING HOME WITH ME ALL THE TIME.

AND EVERY TIME I TRIED TO *TALK* WITH TOMARI-CHAN, SHE SEEMED TO BE BUSY.

DAYS LATER--

TOMARI-CHAN! LET'S EAT LUNCH TOGETHER, OKAY?

WELL...

SORRY, GUYS.

YOU DO HAVE THAT RIGHT, AFTER ALL.

FOR NOW.

I WAS A *REAL BITCH* BACK THERE, WASN'T I?

TO KEEP *RUNNING* LIKE THAT FOREVER.

HOWEVER... I DON'T THINK YOU'LL BE ABLE...

FSHHHHH GAK?!

HERE WE GO! IT'S TIME...

FSHHHHH

FOR SOME PERSONAL PARENTAL LOVE!!

HEH HEH HEH...

AND THAT OTHER...

WHEN I SAW HER THAT TIME...

BUT...

THAT'S WAY TOO SELF-CENTERED OF ME!

HA HA! NO *WAY*!

SHE DIDN'T REALLY LOOK "MAD" AT ME.

IT WAS MORE LIKE SHE WAS ON THE VERGE OF *TEARS*.

ブシ!!
SHOOP

チャ!!

はッ!!じゃ!!
STOMP
CRACKLE

HAZUMU?
AAAARGH!!
I DON'T HAVE
MY GLASSES
ON!! WHERE
ARE MY
GLASSES?!!

ACK!!
MOM! DID
YOU JUST
STEP ON
WHAT I
THINK YOU
DID?!

THAT'S THE ONLY WAY YOU'RE GONNA GET TO BE MY GROOM.

YOU'RE GONNA HAVE TO BE *STRONG* AND *AWESOME* AND *MANLY* FIRST!

HA!

LIKE I'M GONNA LET SOME *PANSY* BE MY GROOM!

I'LL BE YOUR GROOM!

SO *START* ACTING MORE LIKE A *BOY* ALREADY!! AND QUIT MAKIN' DAISY-CHAINS!

AWW...

THAT'S RIGHT.

SHE'S ABSOLUTELY RIGHT.

I... UH...

UM...

I...

I KNOW YOU HAVE TO BE *PRETTY* MAD AT ME...

UM...

MAD? ABOUT *WHAT*?

SO YOU *ARE* MAD?

AND *HURT...*?

WHAT?! SPIT IT OUT ALREADY!

AH HA HA HA...

HOLD ON... GIVE ME A SEC, OKAY?

I DON'T WANT THAT TO DRIVE US APART.

BUT...

UGH...

I WANT US TO BE FRIENDS AGAIN, LIKE WE WERE BEFORE!

I DON'T WANT TO NOT BE ABLE TO TALK TO YOU.

I HATE IT!

HUH ...?

YOU'RE IMPORTANT TO ME, TOMARI-CHAN.

YOU'RE MY FRIEND. I... L--

SMACK!

QUIT SPOUTING *CRAP* LIKE THAT, OKAY?

PHOO PHOO

I MEAN, YOU *LOVE* YASUNA, DON'T YOU?

Gwii...

THAT'S WHY YOU AND HER DID THAT. *RIGHT?!*

DAMMIT! THERE'S NO GETTING OUT OF THIS NOW!

hup

YOU'D DO THE SAME THING FOR US BOTH, RIGHT?

SO... THAT MEANS...

YOU LIKE US *BOTH* THE SAME... RIGHT?

YEAH.

THAT?! B-BUT I-I JUST KINDA SAT THERE, AND Y-YASUNA-CHAN CAME UP, AND-- ARGH!!

ack!

GYAAAA?!

oh jeez!

oh jeez!

GRAB

SAME THING ...?

TOMAR--

MORON...

HEY, YOU KNOW WHAT? I'M A GIRL NOW, SO I REALLY **CAN** BECOME A BRIDE!

ALL RIGHT... ALL RIGHT... I GIVE UP. I'LL ACCEPT IT.

A LOT!!

I LOVE HAZUMU!

JEEZ, IT'S NOT EVEN SUMMER VACATION YET, BUT IT'S ALREADY *SCORCH-ING!*

HEY! NOW *THAT'S* AN IDEA! WHY DON'T WE GO TO THE BEACH?

YEAH. I BET A DIP IN THE OCEAN WOULD FEEL *REAL* GOOD ABOUT NOW.

YEAH! WHY NOT? SUNDAY SOUNDS GOOD. LET'S GO FOR IT!

#9 A Trip to the Beach

JUST AN INNOCENT CONVERSATION BETWEEN GUYS.

IT STARTED OUT SO HARMLESSLY...

#9 A Trip to the Beach

BUT MY BEST FRIEND GOT TURNED INTO A GIRL A LITTLE WHILE AGO.

AND GOING THERE WITH A BUNCH OF GIRLS...

AND GOING TO THE BEACH WITH SOME GUYS...

LONG~

BUSTY

SLEEK~

THE BODY'S CHANGED, BUT THE PERSON'S STILL THE SAME...

stare

ARE JUST TWO TOTALLY DIFFERENT BEASTS!

WHAT'S WRONG?

I CAN'T LET DIRTY THOUGHTS BETRAY THE BOND OF FRIENDSHIP FORGED BETWEEN MEN!!

DUMMY DUMMY

ASUTA?

HAZUMU IS MY BEST FRIEND!

WHOA, WAIT!

WHAT THE HELL AM I THINKING?!

UWAAA AAAA!!

tee hee

why?

B-because..!

N-NO! THAT'S OKAY!

COME SIT WITH US AND TALK.

WHY ARE YOU SITTING OVER HERE ALL BY YOURSELF?

JUST LEMME ALONE!

hee hee

URK

THE PRIMORDIAL SOUP FROM WHICH SPRUNG *ALL* LIFE ON THIS PLANET.

THE OCEAN...

SPLOOT

CO--?!

WITH WHOM SHALL YOU CHOOSE TO PER-FORM?

I'm terribly intrigued...

NO-BODY!!

EVEN NOW, IT EVOKES FEELINGS OF "LOVE" LIKE *FEW* OTHER PLACES ON THIS WORLD.

ACCORDING TO MY DATA, HUMANS BECOME SO OVERWHELMED BY "LOVE" WHEN NEAR THE OCEAN THAT THEY OFTEN *COPULATE* RIGHT UPON ITS SHORES.

GYAAAAARA SHRIP

I SHALL WEAR *THIS* INSTEAD.

MY DOCU-MENTATION HAD IT CATEGORIZED AS "THE HEIGHT OF FASHION." AH WELL...

IS IT?

And I did not purchase it. I made it.

AND WHAT'S UP WITH *THAT* SWIM-SUIT...?

Where did you buy it?

ISN'T THAT JUST A CENTURY OR TWO OUT OF DATE, SENSEI?

SORA-SENSEI, YOU'RE SO... SO... *BOLD!* ♡

I think I've died and gone to heaven...

SENSEI, NO!!!

drip drip

yay!

ZOOOOM

NOW THEN, EVERYONE, TO THE *OCEAN!*

HAZUMU!

HAZUMU-KUN...

SHALL WE GO?

LET'S GO!

I JUST CAN'T CHOOSE BETWEEN THEM.

GRIN

HAZUMU *WOULD* LOOK JUST LIKE ANY OTHER NORMAL GIRL.

TO SOME-ONE WHO DOESN'T KNOW US...

OH YEAH, THAT'S RIGHT.

Shut up creeps!

YOU THINK THAT GUY SHE'S WITH IS HER *BOY-FRIEND?*

UGH!

A HOTTIE LIKE HER IS GOING OUT WITH *THAT?*

CHECK OUT *THAT* CHICK OVER THERE!

Hey!

OOH, NIIICE!

MAKE THAT "LIKE ANY OTHER SUPER-HOT BABE"!!

She's not my girlfriend, she's my best friend... and she used to be a guy...

NO...IT DOESN'T.

?

?

I can just feel the stares of jealousy stabbing into my back!

NYA HA HA HA

WHOA, WAIT...

ASUTA? WHAT THE *HECK* ARE YOU DOING?

N-NO-THING...

?

LET'S GET BACK TO THE OTHERS, THEN!

DOESN'T THIS MEAN I *WIN?!*

ASUTA! WHERE ARE YOU GOING?!

WAY PAST *EVERYBODY*, ACTUALLY.

WHERE--?

WE'VE GONE *WAY* PAST WHERE THE OTHERS ARE.

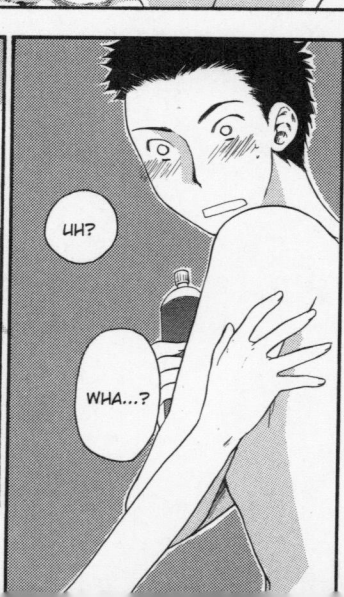

UH?

WHA...?

HRM...

NOBODY ...?

PUU?

WILL ONE MAKE A MOVE?

OH...

SENSEI! ♡

YES?

EEE! ♡

THERE'S *NOBODY* OUT THIS WAY AT ALL.

NOW, FINALLY... FINALLY! THE TIME HAS COME FOR ME TO PUT AN END TO THE WAITING!

BUT

I, TSUKI NAMIKO, HAVE BEEN TRAPPED IN A BOYFRIEND-LESS *LIMBO* FOR ALL 35 YEARS OF MY LIFE.

UM...

YASUNA?

YES?

YOU KNOW, ABOUT...

Hazumu-Kun is taking an awfully long time...

....

YOU'VE...

BEEN ACTING WEIRD ALL DAY.

ASUTA, WHAT'S GOTTEN INTO *YOU*?

LIKE *HELL* IT'S EMBARRASSING!!

GRAB

MAYBE EVEN A LITTLE... *DISGUSTING.*

YOU'RE STUCK HANGING OUT WITH ME, ISN'T IT?

IT'S BE- CAUSE...

IT MUST BE *EMBARRASSING,* BEING AROUND ME NOW.

HUH...?

HAZUMU.

I-I...

PULL

I THINK I'M...

FALLING--

IT WAS SO FRAIL, SO *WEAK*...

#10 I'll Just Watch...

SEE, AYUKI? WATCH.

SEE HOW HARD THE PUPA IS WORKING TO BECOME A BUTTERFLY?

ONE DAY, YOU'LL TURN INTO A *BEAUTIFUL* BUTTERFLY AND SPREAD YOUR WINGS TO FLY AWAY.

YOU'RE JUST LIKE THAT LITTLE PUPA, AYUKI.

IT'S SO *BEAUTIFUL*.

NO. THAT'S OKAY.

I DON'T CARE IF I DON'T GET TO BE A BUTTERFLY.

YET...

#10 I'll Just Watch...

I AM EXPECTING GREAT THINGS OF YOU... ALL OF YOU.

He's looking right at me...

SIGH

THUD

AW, MAN!!

HECK YEAH! YOU SHOULD'VE SEEN IT WHEN WE'D GO TO HAUNTED HOUSES. HAZUMU'S *UNBELIEVABLE!*

Snicker

WHAT?!

I HATE *DARES!* I HATE 'EM, HATE 'EM, HATE 'EM!!

YEAH, I MEAN, YOU ALWAYS *DID* MAKE MOST SCAREDY-CATS LOOK BRAVE.

REALLY?

HAZUMU? "UNBELIEV-ABLE"?!

HEY! TOMARI-CHAN! KNOCK IT OFF!

AH HA HA HA HA HA HA

HAZUMU-KUN?

There, it's not so scary when we're together, now is it?

Hush, now. No need to be afraid.

Oh, Asuta! I'm so scared!

SHE'D GRAB ONTO ME AND STICK THERE LIKE GLUE! YOU COULDN'T HAVE GOTTEN HER OFF ME WITH A CROWBAR!

!!

squeeze squeeze

SNORT

NYA HA HA HA HA HA HA HA

BY THE WAY, THIS IS WHAT REALLY HAPPENS...

Dammit, Hazumu!

Quit pulling already! You'll tear my dress!

LET'S GO TOGETHER, HAZUMU-KUN. WOULDN'T THAT BE FUN?

Well... uh... O-OKAY. WE'RE IN THE SAME GROUP AND ALL...

WOP

Yammer Yammer

Hee hee.

Me too!

·····

·····

NOR DO I EVER INTEND TO START.

ALL RIGHT, ALL MY *LOVELY* STUDENTS!! THE *ABSOLUTELY AMAZING* DARE YOU'VE ALL BEEN WAITING FOR SO *ANXIOUSLY* IS JUST ABOUT TO BEGIN! ♡

THE FINISH LINE IS IN FRONT OF THE GYMNASIUM! ♡

READY! SET! GOOOO!! ♡

I'm scared already!

Waaah!

Puu!

their piece of paper? Perfect! Each group will go to the room listed...

prove they were there, and then come back outside.

Does everyone have...

WE'LL GET THROUGH THIS ALL RIGHT IF WE TRY, RIGHT, HAZUMU-KUN?

UM...

YEAH...

HM?

TEE HEE HEE! ♡ NOW THAT WE'RE ALL *ALONE* TOGETH--

SORA-SENSEI!!

SORA-SENSEI?

EEK!

SWP

AAAHHH!

AFH!

YAA!

tmp

HM... THAT METHOD FAILED...

shf shf shf shf shf

TWITCH

unfortunate

KMAAAA AAAAAAAA

HAZUMU!!

HAZUMU-KUN?!

HAZUMU!!

HAZUMU-KUN!

?

KYAAAAAAA!

Come, darling

AWESOME! I'M HERE FOR YOU, HAZUMU! COME, RUN INTO MY ARMS!

OH, ASUTA!

HAZUMU?!

A-

AYUKI-
CHAN...?

SQUISH

I JUST WANTED TO WATCH.

...I USED TO *LOVE* WATCHING CATERPILLARS LEAVE THEIR CHRYSALLIS AND TURN INTO BUTTERFLIES.

THE JUST-BORN WINGS WERE *STILL* PEARLY WHITE...

AND LET THEM GRADUALLY DRY INTO BEAUTIFUL, BRIGHT PATTERNS.

SLOWLY AND PAINFULLY, THEY'D SPREAD THEIR WINGS...

BUT I *NEVER* ONCE THOUGHT THAT I WOULD WANT TO TRANS-FORM LIKE A BUTTERFLY...

OR DANCE THROUGH THE SKY ON MY OWN COLORFUL WINGS.

AND SO FRAGILE THAT ANY STRAIN WOULD TEAR THEM.

THAT BY ITSELF IS *ENOUGH* FOR ME.

IT WAS SO *BEAUTIFUL.*

DON'T HURRY YOURSELF. TAKE YOUR TIME IN CHOOSING BETWEEN YASUNA AND TOMARI.

SLOWLY AND CAREFULLY, SO THAT YOU DON'T TEAR YOUR NEWBORN WINGS.

HOW INTRIGU-ING.

THERE IS *MUCH* MORE TO THIS...

THAN IT WOULD APPEAR AT FIRST GLANCE.

SENSEI?!

SORA-SENSEI!!

Let's go home!

Yeah, let's.

· · · · · · · ·

THUD

HAZU-MUUU!! I'LL SAVE YOUUU!!

WHAAA?!

WHERE ARE YO--?!

WHUMP

CRASH

HAZUMU-
KUN...

#11 The Princess of Curry

I WANT
YOU TO
ALWAYS
SMILE
FOR ME.

I WANT
YOU TO
BE *MINE*.

BUT...

#11 The Princess of Curry

WELL, "GARDENING CLUB" IS JUST OUR OFFICIAL NAME. IN REALITY, WE'RE MORE OF A HORTICULTURE CLUB.

CARROTS, POTATOES AND ONIONS!

THEY'RE SOME OF THE VEGETABLES MY CLUB RAISED!

WE DO JUST ABOUT ANY-THING THAT INVOLVES PLANTS.

HOW WONDERFUL! I DIDN'T KNOW THE GARDENING CLUB ALSO DID VEGATABLES.

CURRY?

HA HA! YEP! AND THEY'RE ALSO THE INGREDI-ENTS FOR CURRY!

CARROTS... POTATOES...

HMM... NOW THAT'S AN IDEA...

DO YOU WANT TO TAKE SOME HOME?

HUH?

HAZUMU-KUN...

HOW ABOUT WE TAKE ALL OF THESE AND HOLD A CURRY-PARTY AT MY HOUSE?

YEAH. DO YOU WANT TO GO WITH US?

PUUUUU! ♡

JAN-PUU LOVES CURRY!

MAMA-SAMA MADE MILD CURRY! IT WAS SUPER *PUUMMY!* ♡

PUUU→♡

OF COURSE.

WOULD YOU LIKE TO COME TOO...?

ピ〜ンポ〜ン
DINGDONG

WHY, HELLO THERE.

OH, THIS MUST BE THE COUSIN YOU TOLD ME ABOUT YESTERDAY...

YOU'RE JAN-PUU-CHAN, CORRECT?

WEL-COME.

And Sensei, of course.

PUUU! ♥

YASUNAN! ♥

UH... H-HI.

GYAAAAA

HELLO, ALL! YOU'RE QUITE LATE!

HURG

YEEEEE! SENSEI! EEEEEEEEEEEE

SENSEI, PLEASE! DON'T TURN AROUND!!

WAAAAAA

WE HAVE ALREADY BEGUN COOKING. COME IN AND HELP.

SORA-SENSEI?!

PERSONALLY, BETWEEN THE TWO OF THEM, I'D TAKE HAZUM--

REALLY? I DUNNO...

HM?

HEY, ASUTA? ABOUT YASUNA...

SHE'S REALLY... FEMININE, YOU KNOW?

VRK

Shake Shake

GUYS LIKE HER TYPE...

INSTEAD OF... OTHERS, DON'T THEY?

PLOP

PLOP PLOP

CHOP

CRUMBLE CRUMBLE

REALLY?! CAN I?

TOMARI! IF YOU VALUE YOUR LIFE, DO IT YOURSELF!!

AYUKI, WHY DON'T YOU DO THIS AFTER ALL...?

THEY ARE ALL *WONDERFUL*... BUT THERE IS ANOTHER *DIFFERENT* HAZUMU-KUN...

IS SUCH A FRAIDY-CAT.

HAZUMU-KUN'S BIGGEST, BRIGHTEST SMILE...

SHE LOOKS AT ME LIKE SHE'S UNSURE OF WHAT TO DO.

TALKS TO HER FAVORITE PLANTS...

THE HAZUMU-KUN WHO...

IS SOMETHING SHE ONLY SHARES WHEN *EVERYONE* IS TOGETHER.

ONE THAT I WILL NEVER, EVER SEE BY MYSELF.

AND YOUR WONDERFUL, BRILLIANT SMILE.

YOU, WHO ARE MORE PRECIOUS TO ME THAN ANYTHING...

IT'S ONLY FAIR. I'VE ALWAYS CALLED YOU BY YOUR FIRST NAME.

CALL ME "TOMARI."

HMM?

"TOMARI."

#12 Of Summer Festivals and Cotton Candy

HAZUMU, ARE YOU GOING TO GO TO TONIGHT'S FESTIVAL, DEAR?

mmm!

Toast with bacon and eggs.

PUU? WHAT'S A *"FESTIVAL"*?

nod nod nod

UH-HUH!

FESTIVAL...? *OH!* KASHIMA SHRINE'S SUMMER FESTIVAL, RIGHT?

SLOP PLOP PLOP

ZWSH

UM... WELL... THERE ARE *LOTS* OF FOOD VENDORS WITH THE *BEST* JUNK FOOD, AND THERE ARE *GAME* BOOTHS ALL OVER THE PLACE...

PUUUU!!

AND THERE ARE LOADS OF OTHER THINGS TOO! WANNA COME? IT'S A LOT OF FUN!

WOW, IS IT THAT TIME OF YEAR *ALREADY?*

Especially in THAT outfit!!

W-W-WHAT THE HECK ARE YOU DOING OUT HERE?!

SHH!! RELAX. I AM VISIBLE ONLY TO YOU. AS FOR YOUR QUESTION...

YEEP!

AN OBSERVATION...?

I AM IN THE MIDST OF AN OBSERVATION.

. . . .

!!!!

MAKIN' OUT

OOOH

TEE HEE

OH WELL. NEVERMIND THAT. WHAT IS WRONG?

YOUR EMOTIONAL STATE APPEARS **UNBALANCED.**

P-P-P-PEEPING IS A CRIME!!!

IT IS...?

IT WON'T BE LONG...

I CAN'T KEEP BEING SO SELFISH...

BEFORE THE DAY COMES WHEN I HAVE TO CHOOSE ONE *OVER* THE OTHER.

STRINGING BOTH OF THEM ALONG. BECAUSE I'M TOO SCARED TO MAKE A DECISION.

BUT...

EVEN *CAPABLE* OF MAKING THAT DECISION?

AM I...

I STILL DON'T *EVEN* KNOW WHAT LOVE REALLY IS.

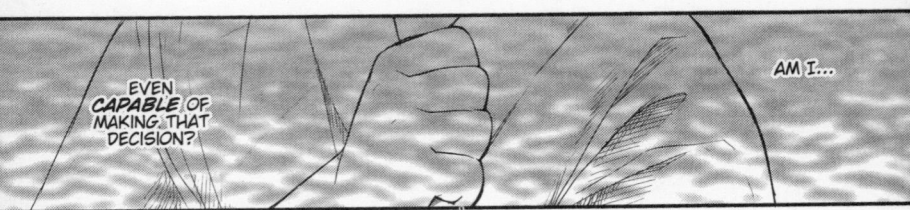

IS IT THE *DESIRE* TO BE WITH HER ALWAYS?

IS IT THE FEELING OF *EXCITE-MENT* WHEN I'M AROUND HER?

WHAT IS *LOVE*?

GOD...

#13 A Little Storm

DON'T WORRY, ASUTA. I'VE STILL GOT TO COME FOR CLUB, SO YOU WON'T BE ALL ALONE.
OH? SO YOU'RE BUSY THIS SUMMER, THEN?
HAZUMU
NO, NOT REALLY. IT'S NOT LIKE I HAVE TO COME EVERY DAY.
whew
OH. THAT'S GOOD...
......
YAAAAAA!!
ka ka ka ka ka ka
heh heh heh
SAY, EVERYONE...!
WHY DON'T WE ALL VISIT THIS PLACE SOMETIME?
SEASIDE PARK

SEASIDE PARK

AN AQUARIUM?

OPENING DAY IS THE DAY AFTER TOMORROW.

AWESOME!

YOU'RE COMING TOO, RIGHT, ASUTA?

CAN'T. SUMMER CLASSES START THAT DAY.

WHAT?! THEY'RE GIVING AWAY MARIN-CHAN CELLPHONE STRAPS TO THE FIRST VISITORS ON OPENING DAY?!

SO, LET'S GO THEN.

I SOOO WANT ONE!

OH YEAH! I'VE SEEN THIS BEFORE! IT WAS ON TV.

ONE THAT'S BEEN MESHED WITH AN AMUSE-MENT PARK, ACCORDING TO THE FLYER.

SURE, I'LL GO!

NOW THAT'S JUST CRUEL!!

OH WELL. NO BIG LOSS.

HAZUMUUU!

I'LL BUY YOU SOMETHING FROM THE GIFT SHOP.

tee hee ♥

FRIENDSHIP

TOMARI-CHAN?

HUH?

OH. YEAH, RIGHT. CAN'T WAIT.

WOO HOO!

WE CAN TURN IT INTO A GIRLS' DAY OUT.

heh heh

?

......

HAZUMUUU...

I CAN'T WAIT! HOW ABOUT YOU, TOMARI-CHAN?

HN.

UM... TOMARI-SAN...?

HN?

I HOPE WE HAVE FUN TOGETHER ON OUR TRIP...

HUH?

OUR TRIP THE DAY AFTER TOMORROW. REMEMBER?

WHA~~?!!

SOMEBODY EXPLAIN TO ME WHY HER REACTION IS SO *DIFFERENT* FROM WHEN I SAID *I* COULDN'T COME!

Aww, why not?! Come on!

HAZUMUU!

boo...

YOU CAN'T COOOME?!

OH... OKAY...

BUT WHEN YOU GET BACK, WE'LL HAVE TO GO AGAIN... *TOGETHER!*

JUST GO ON WITHOUT ME. I DON'T MIND.

WELL, YOU *REALLY* WANT THAT CELLPHONE STRAP, RIGHT?

God, is it ever going to be harsh...

I DON'T HAVE MUCH OF A CHOICE... IT'S A FIVE-DAY OVERNIGHT CAMP.

THAT'S SOOOO UNFAIR!

THMPA
THMPA

Y-YEAH... OKAY...

• • • • • • • •

IT'S BEEN AGES...

SINCE I LAST...

WALKED HOME BY MYSELF...

I'm so dead!

ouch

TOMARI-
CHA--

HM...?
FROM AYUKI?

brrrng

WHAT COULD SHE WANT?

"SORRY."

"SOMETHING CAME UP."

BRRRRRNG

WHAT?!

P1

SQUEEZE

"HAZUMU-KUN IS GOING TO BE LEFT ALONE WITH YASUNA!"

"FORGIVE ME!"

....

....

……………

……………

TOMARI-CHAN...

EVEN THOUGH I WASN'T *THERE*.

SHE LOOKED LIKE SHE WAS HAVING *LOADS* OF FUN...

SHE WAS LAUGHING.

HAZUMU-KUN.

I'M SORRY I KEPT YOU WAITING.

ARE YOU FEELING A LITTLE TIRED?

HUH...?

OH... UH, NO... NOT REALLY.

#14 Tomari and...

YASUNA-CHAN...

SHE WAS ALWAYS SO BEAUTIFUL, SO NICE.

WHEN SHE SMILED, IT WAS LIKE THE BLOOMING OF A FLOWER.

YASUNA-CHAN...

HAVE HER SMILE AT ME MORE...

TALK WITH HER MORE...

I JUST WANTED TO BE AROUND HER MORE...

ドキ
バ

I NEVER KNEW...

THUMP

LIPS COULD BE SO WARM...

BATHUMP

BATHUMP

BATHUMP

SHE'S THE FIRST GIRL I EVER FELL IN LOVE WITH.

K-KLAK

K-KLAK

HA!

FWEEEET

ANOTHER LAP!

SHF SHF

deep breath

WELL... I'M HERE.

B-THUMP

B-THUMP

WHAT HAPPENED...?

YOU KNOW...

......

SHE'S SO PRIM AND PROPER, SO LOVELY AND NICE.

YASUNA IS LIKE THE *PERFECT* GIRL. LOOK UP "FEMININE" IN THE DICTIONARY, AND YOU'D FIND HER PICTURE.

I'M...

BUT...

NOT LIKE HER.

UM...

I'M NOT PRETTY, OR PROPER.

WELL...

BUT I'M OKAY.
I MEAN, IT'S NOT LIKE THERE'S ANY HOPE I'LL GET TURNED BACK, ANYWAY.
AND ALL MY FRIENDS TREAT ME LIKE THEY ALWAYS DID, SO I CAN *DEAL* WITH IT.
HAZUMU!
SEE?
blush
YEAH... I SEE...
IT'S... IT'S *WONDERFUL* HAVING A DAUGHTER.
NO.
YOU STAY OVER HERE.
HUH?
YOU'D WRECK THE PICTURE.
WHA?!!
CUTENESS IS EVERYTHING!!

sneak sneak

Because Jan-puu really, really, really wanted to play with Onee-nii-sama today!

In the end, Jan-puu didn't ask Master for permission to leave.

PUU!

PUU.

JEEZ.

AND THANKS TO THAT, I'M THE **ONLY** GUY LEFT IN THE CLUB.

But Jan-puu thinks...

Onee-nii-sama has lots and lots of friends besides Tomarin and Yasunan.

BUT HAZUMU-SEMPAI WAS **ALWAYS** CUTER THAN OTHER GIRLS, EVEN WHEN SHE WAS A BOY!

that Onee-nii-sama all by herself is good enough.

They all get along super well.

C'MON GUYS, KNOCK IT OFF... PLEASE...?

ガボガボ BLURBLE BLURBLE BLURBLE
MMPH...
OSARAGI!!
OH MY GOD!
KYAAA
HAZUMU-KUN!
PU...
PU...
PUUUUUUUUU!!

PUU!

#15 The One I Love Is...

SNAP

PUU~

ONEE-NII-SAMA... EVER SINCE THAT NIGHT IN THE WOODS, ONEE-NII-SAMA LOOKS HAPPIEST WHEN TALKING ON THE CELLPHONE WITH TOMARIN.

N-NOT REALLY! I SWEAR!

CHOMP

I DO...?

O-OH?

PUU~!

UM,
HAZUMU?

TODAY...
AFTER SCHOOL,
DO YOU WANT
TO GO TO THAT
AQUARIUM
AMUSEMENT
PARK PLACE?

HM...?

I MEAN,
I DON'T HAVE
TRACK TODAY,
AND I COULDN'T
GO WHEN YOU
WENT THE *LAST*
TIME. AND...

I WANT
IT TO BE
JUST THE
TWO OF US
GOING.

SURE!

O-OKAY!

GOOD MORNING.

ピゥ ワゥゥ

YEEK!

G—

GOOD MORNING!

AH!!

WHRL

WHAT'S WRONG?

N—

NOTHING! NOTHING AT ALL! EVERYTHING'S FINE!

KOFF

IS IT JUST ME, OR IS THERE SOME-THING REALLY *WEIRD* GOING ON HERE...?

IT'S ONLY FAIR. I HAD YOU ALL TO MYSELF FOR A DAY, ONCE...

IT'S OKAY. I DON'T MIND.

GO HAVE FUN.

#16 Because I Like You

HAZUMU-KUN...

I MUST'VE IMAGINED IT.

NEVER MIND.

HM?

HAZUMU? SOMETHING WRONG?

NOT REALLY... I JUST THOUGHT I HEARD...

#16 Because I Like You

OH MY GOD! THEY'RE *HUGE!*

YEAH! WOW! THEY REALLY ARE!

I COULDN'T STOP THINKING ABOUT YOU, TOMARI-CHAN...

WHY?

BUT I KINDA DON'T REMEMBER THE FIRST TIME TOO MUCH...

WELL... YEAH...

HUH? WHY ARE YOU SURPRISED? ISN'T THIS YOUR *SECOND* TIME HERE?

STEAM STEAM

WHAT THE HELL ARE YOU SAYING?!

MORON!!

OH... UM... SORRY.

HUH?

...SO EVEN THOUGH I WAS LOOKING AT ALL THIS STUFF, I WASN'T *REALLY* SEEING IT, YOU KNOW...?

かぁ

BLUSH

BTHMP

BTHMP

PEEK

BLUSH

PEEK

BLUSH

HMM?

NAMIKO-EYE VISION

K-SHIK

S-S-S-SORA-SEN-SEII!!!

VWOOOOM

VNNN III // /'/ YY

HAZUMU-
KUN...

HFF

HFF

ヒョPI
Iy

GO
HAVE
FUN.

IT'S
OKAY.
I DON'T
MIND.

I THOUGHT THAT I DIDN'T MIND BEING ALONE.

I NEVER REALLY GOT ALONG WELL WITH OTHER PEOPLE, EVEN WHEN I WAS STILL A LITTLE CHILD.

I COULDN'T EVEN SEE THE BOYS IN MY CLASS, AND THE GIRLS WHO COULD PLAY AND INTERACT WITH THEM WERE JUST... DIFFERENT... TO ME.

SO I STAYED BY MYSELF.

NOW, LOOKING BACK, I THINK I JUST DIDN'T KNOW THE REAL MEANING OF THE WORD "ALONE."

NOT UNTIL I MET YOU.

HEY...

YOU KNOW KAMIIZUMI-SAN?

YEAH. SHE'S REALLY HARD TO GET CLOSE TO, YOU KNOW?

SHE ACTS LIKE SHE CAN'T EVEN BE *BOTHERED* WITH THE LIKES OF US.

EXACTLY! SHE'S COLD LIKE THAT.

THERE! HOW DOES THAT FEEL?

WAS THE WATER *GOOD?* I BET IT WAS!

· · · · · · ·

THAT'S SO *WEIRD...*

IT'S NOT LIKE ANYONE COULD EVER UNDERSTAND WHAT A PLANT FEELS.

A BOY...?

HE'S *TALKING* WITH THE PLANTS? EVEN HAVING A CONVERSATION WITH THEM!

Well, there's plenty more for you!

YOU'LL GET YOUR TURN IN JUST A MINUTE!

OH, *SORRY!* I DIDN'T FORGET YOU. *HONEST!*

WHAT'S THAT?

THE
BREEZE...
IT FEELS
SO KIND...

WHAT
IS THIS
STRANGE
FEELING?

HMM?

BLUSH

WHAT IS
THIS ODD
FEELING
NAGGING
ME...?

I WANT
TO KNOW
MORE ABOUT
THAT BOY.

I'M SO...
EMBARRASSED!

BUT *WHY*?

I'VE NEVER
BEEN EMBAR-
RASSED ABOUT
ANYTHING
BEFORE.

DASH

AH...!

I WANT TO LIVE TOGETHER WITH YOU, IN THIS WORLD.

LIKE THE PLANTS THAT GROW LUSCIOUS AND GREEN IN THE LIGHT OF YOUR LOVE, I WANT TO STAY BY YOUR SIDE AND BASK.

BUT...

ZING

ズ

キ

ッ

IF THAT'S WHAT WILL MAKE HAZUMU-KUN HAPPY...

IF THAT'S WHAT HAZUMU-KUN WANTS...

THEN I...

HUFF HUFF

-MU... -KUN...

#17 Walls

K-KLAK

K-KLAK

K-KLAK

K-KLAK

YASUNA-CHAN...

SQUEEZE

THEN YASUNA-CHAN WOULD *NEVER* HAVE COLLAPSED.

Go have fun.

It's okay, I don't mind.

IF ONLY I HAD PAID MORE ATTENTION!

YASUNA-CHAN...

HA
HA
HA
HA!

TO EVERYONE, YASUNA-CHAN WAS SOMEONE... DIFFERENT.

BACK THEN...

EVEN... NO...

ESPECIALLY TO ME.

YOU GUYS AREN'T LOOKING SO GOOD...

HMM...

I CAN'T WATER YOU ANYMORE EITHER...

HMM. WHAT ELSE CAN I DO...?

SHE WAS SO BEAUTIFUL, SO ELEGANT.

UNTIL *THAT* DAY.

BUT SHE ALWAYS HAD THIS AURA OF COLD INDIFFERENCE AROUND HER.

I HAD BELIEVED SHE BELONGED TO A WORLD FAR, FAR AWAY FROM MY OWN...

KAMIIZUMI-SAN!

OVER TIME, I CAME TO KNOW THE REAL YASUNA-CHAN.

I STARTED TO FALL IN LOVE.

IT WAS THE FIRST TIME I'D EVER HAD A CRUSH ON ANYONE.

KLAK

KLAK

AFTER WHAT HAPPENED *THAT* AFTERNOON...

I WENT HIKING IN THE MOUNTAINS TO TRY TO FORGET EVERYTHING.

MY THOUGHTS OF HER, MY PAIN, MY FEARS...

I TRIED TO RUN AWAY FROM IT ALL.

TURNED INTO SOMETHING ELSE ENTIRELY. BODY, HEART AND MIND...

IF I COULD BE CHANGED, I THOUGHT...

EVERYTHING WOULD BE SO MUCH EASIER.

BUT YOU... YOU ALWAYS LOOKED STRAIGHT AT ME.

THANK YOU.

I APPRE- CIATE YOU COMING TO SEE ME...

SO IT'S BEGUN.

NO...

·······

IT HAD *ALREADY* BEGUN.

I'M SURE THIS IS JUST ANOTHER STEP IN THE RIGHT DIRECTION...

HMM.

THERE ISN'T MUCH TIME LEFT...

IS THERE?

THE SUMMER'S ALMOST OVER...

SLUURP

SIIIP

THOUGH IT'S STILL REALLY, REALLY, REALLY, REALLY HOT OUTSIDE...

YES. SUMMER IS ONLY OVER ACCORDING TO THE CALENDAR...

SLUURP

SIIIP

#18 Of People, Dreams, Fireworks, and Hopelessness

HUH?

OH...! NO, NO, I'M NOT BEING *JEALOUS* OR ANYTHING.

hee hee

YOU TWO ARE *SO* LUCKY.

IT'S JUST YOU TWO HAVE BEEN FRIENDS FOR YEARS. YOU MUST SHARE SO MANY MEMORIES.

IT MUST BE NICE, HAVING THAT.

Hee hee

LUCKY.

WELL... YEAH...

WE DO KINDA HAVE A LOT OF THEM...

MEMORIES...

#18 Of People, Dreams, Fireworks, and Hopelessness

HAZUMU,
LET'S DO
THESE
NEXT.

OKAY!

OVER
HERE! WE'RE
GONNA DO
SPARKLERS!

HEY,
YASUNA-
CHAN!

I'LL GO GET ANOTHER PACK!

SWSH SWSH

TOMARI-SAN...?

HM?

THANK YOU... FOR THE OTHER DAY.

IT'S AN OFFER OF ALLIANCE.

BUT THIS TIME...

LAST TIME, I DECLARED WAR ON YOU.

TOGETHER, WE CAN'T LOSE.

EXACTLY.

Special #2

ONE MAN'S DARING MISSION: INVADE THE PAJAMA PARTY!

THAT PAJAMA PARTY!!

I *WILL* ATTEND...

EIGHT HOURS EARLIER...

EVER SINCE I *GOT* TURNED INTO A GIRL, THERE'S ONE THING I'VE BEEN *DYING* TO DO!

YOU KNOW...

WELL...

WHAT'S THAT?

HM?

OH YEAH...

LET'S DO IT AT MY HOUSE, THEN!

ASUTA, DO YOU WANT TO...

YOU BET! ♥

UM... WHAT SHE SAID.

SORRY! ♥

HAZUMU~!

hee hee ♥

HAZUMU-KUN...

...COME?

PAJAMA PARTIES ARE FOR *GIRLS* ONLY.

WHAP

MEEP!

DAAARGH!!

I THINK NOT!!

AH!

GOD...!

DRAG DRAG

SLUMP

MMPH...

W-WAIT! DON'T FORGET M--!

SLAM

FLOWERS & PLANTS
OF KASHIMASHI

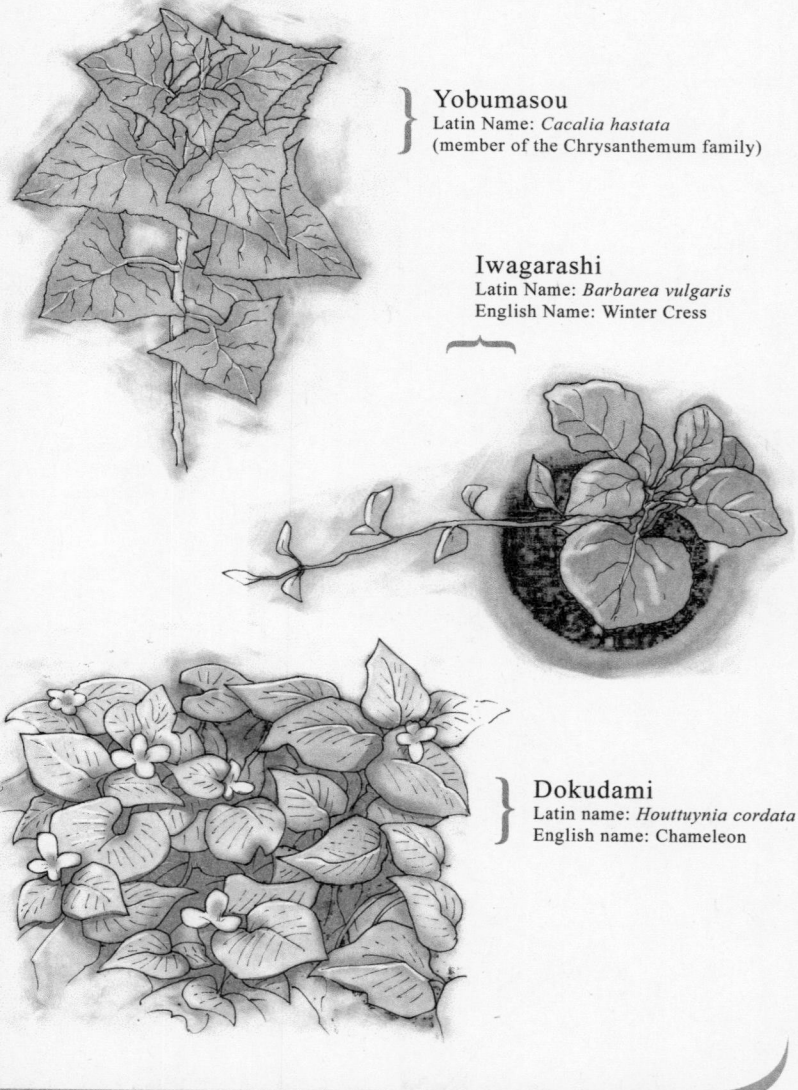

Yobumasou
Latin Name: *Cacalia hastata*
(member of the Chrysanthemum family)

Iwagarashi
Latin Name: *Barbarea vulgaris*
English Name: Winter Cress

Dokudami
Latin name: *Houttuynia cordata*
English name: Chameleon

Momijigasa
Latin name: *Cacalia delphiniifolia*
(Type of Cacalia)

Fuki
Latin Name: *Petasites japonicus*
English Name: Butterbur

Kaki
Latin: *Diospyros kaki*
Name: Persimmon Tree

THE END

YOU'RE READING THE WRONG WAY

This is the last page of
Kashimashi Omnibus Collection 1

This book reads from right to left, Japanese style. To read from the beginning, flip the book over to the other side, start with the top right panel, and take it from there.

If this is your first time reading manga, just follow the diagram. It may seem backwards at first, but you'll get used to it! Have fun!